No Parachutes to Carry Me Home

Maisha Z. Johnson

Punk ✈ Hostage ✈ Press

NO PARACHUTES TO CARRY ME HOME
MAISHA Z JOHNSON

© Maisha Z Johnson 2015

ISBN-10: 1-940213-83-5
ISBN-13: 978-1-940213-83-5

Punk Hostage Press
P.O. Box 1869
Hollywood CA, 90078
www.punkhostagepress.com

Editor: A. Razor

Introduction: Sandra Alcosser

Cover Design: Geoff Melville

Editor's Acknowledgements

When we started Punk Hostage Press we wanted to be able to create a space where we could watch writers and poets who were already empowering themselves within a positive community put out their best work with us and create new connections to new voices through the whole process. At the San Francisco book release of Hollie Hardy's *How To Take A Bullet and other Survival Poems,* Hollie had enlisted some of her favorite poets to read so as to make it a celebration of her new book with her community. The event was a success and in the course of the evening while talking with Maisha Z Johnson, who had read her work that night as part of the event, Maisha revealed that she had a manuscript she had been working on as well. Of course, we asked if she would consider letting us see her book and, if we felt it was right for us, if she would consider publishing it with Punk Hostage Press. She obliged, and this was a collection of her work that was noteworthy from beginning to end in such a way that we immediately made an offer to publish it as a book of poems. We are so grateful that Maisha agreed to work with us on putting out this book and this is exemplary of the organic process that exists in the power of the word, of the poetry.

I worked on the book's layout and read it over and over, marveling at its voice, its dynamic and the stories that these poems tell. I played with several graphics for the cover, finally collaborating with Geoff Melville on the finished design. We wanted something that was both colorful and celebratory, but also spoke of the longing blues of identity that the title implied.

Maisha's work stands out as an important illumination on identities and the multifaceted universe they speak to. Here is blackness, queerness, empowerment, human migration, traumatization, politics of power, personage of all this and a mystical soulfulness combined. There are poems of origin that outline the way we store our memories in all our senses. There are stories of raw beauty and passionate survival. Maisha is an advocate for social justice and the acknowledgement of our empirical knowledge of who we are, who we want to be, who can be.

We would like to thank all of those in our community who have shown support for the efforts of making this book come to fruition. Sandra Alcosser for the brilliant introduction to this collection. Kwame Dawes, Toni Mirosevich and Ellen Bass for reading the proof and giving their quoted remarks to the effort. Kwan Booth for his feedback and support. All the Punk Hostage Press and Words As Works family as well as the Bay Area literary community that is a fertile ground for the profound beauty it inspires such as this book here. We are forever grateful for you all.

- A. Razor, 2015

Introduction

Maisha Z. Johnson's elegant meditation on human difference, *No Parachutes to Carry Me Home*, opens with an epigraph from June Jordan's *On the Black Family* –

we came and we come in a glory of darkness
around the true reasons for sharing
our dark and our beautiful
name

As though in direct response to this testament, readers are introduced to the compassionate speaker of the opening poem *Sacrifices* who will guide us through the book and the life of its protagonist. This neighbor-- the book's witness-- describes the unsmiling stone face of an angel on her stoop and the anonymous sacrifices that are lit and left at the angel's feet. She concludes:

i like to imagine these sacrifices
as somebody's secret – someone
who spends his evenings making promises
to his family. nights, asking my angel for the same.

The narrator of *No Parachutes* is not a shadow spying from behind the curtains, but a woman who goes forth each day to imagine the suffering of others not so different from her own.

We partake in one initiation after another, as she moves from the loss of a young girl's magic marble to her first sexual experience with another woman. Throughout there is a dialogical tension between external and internal reality which the speaker must true the way one true's the bubble in a level or the sharpness of a blade.

i knew the answer
to the true or false question,
and i knew *my* answer—
the two were not the same.

From *mr. lowell's religion class, st. mary's high school*

And she knows that her answers are not without consequence:

god sat at the edge
of my desk, her gray dreadlocks
dipped in ink black as my pupils

There is a humorous counterpoint, a leitmotif that runs through the book, surely the voice of the superego reminding the narrator how she might be perceived by others. These poems are all titled *the people say* and the people say things like *black girls don't do yoga*. The people say *black girls don't kiss dogs. Black girls don't have eating disorders.*

And yet we know, like the speaker in the poet's chosen epigraph by Gwendolyn Brooks from *a song in the front yard*, Maisha Z. Johnson will not be shaped by what the people say, nor will she be detoured by her

vi

own mistakes. She will move from the front yard, from the boredom of the beautiful, to the untended out back.

> I've stayed in the front yard all my life.
> I want a peek at the back
> Where it's rough and untended and hungry weed grows.
> A girl gets sick of a rose.

Gwendolyn Brooks, *a song in the front yard*

She will explore her parental homeland with nostalgia and curiosity.

> i wish this map would show
> where the queer girls go. in places
> of pretending those girls don't exist,
> they hold each other
> somewhere, perhaps in plain sight.

A reader cannot help but love the narrator of this first powerful collection of poems as she enters one life, then another, from Trinidad to Oakland, and approaches each with her great gifts of simple clarity , lyric beauty and humility--

> me, carrying only my gentle breath beneath
> loose jeans and a baggy black sweatshirt.

Sandra Alcosser, poet, *A Fish to Feed All Hunger* and *Except by Nature*

Acknowledgments for *No Parachutes to Carry Me Home*

"island's daughter" – published in Eleven Eleven, nominated for a Pushcart Prize

"Before We Know" – published in aaduna

"Shades of Nude" – published in aaduna, nominated for a Pushcart Prize

"mr. lowell's religion class, st. mary's high school" – published in Blackberry: A Magazine

"remember tonight" – published in As/Us

"the people say" p. 14 – published in Tandem Vol. 2

"your cat speaks of sadness" – published in Samizdat Literary Journal

"mari goes home" – published in Matrices: Origins

"island home" – published in sParkle & bLink

"chapped lips" – published in Saturday Night Special Anniversary Anthology Zine

TABLE OF CONTENTS

All my thanks for my family, especially Mom and Dad, for the wave of support this book rides in on.

And to my boo, Kwan Booth, for the groovy rhythm you give to my heart.

Sacrifices

we came and we come in a glory of darkness
around the true reasons for sharing
our dark and our beautiful
name

June Jordan, *On the Black Family*

sacrifices

someone is making sacrifices
to the angel statue on my front step.

i never find the offerings intact.
some mornings, i see only
ashes blackening her feet,
and the distant smell of burning paper
is what remains of whatever went up in flames.
on other days, the sunlight bounces
from chicken bones crisscrossed and clean,
as if the raccoons washed them after eating.

these days, it could be anyone
turning to her unsmiling, stone face
for help. the desperation leaves no fingerprint.
i like to imagine these sacrifices
as somebody's secret – someone
who spends his evenings making promises
to his family. nights, asking my angel for the same.

island's daughter

i know the land only as my fingertips trace it,
dotted roads puttering into Tunapuna.
town of my father's birth rests
between market tents, white and puffy,
drawn like parachutes just landed
    on this map of Trinidad.

    i wish this map would show
the highest tree my father climbed
as a boy. let me ascend,
meet the dare his small feet left there,
and recover the prints
he resolved to leave behind.
i should know all he knows, i say,
while his distance disagrees. let my feet
unveil what he won't reveal to me.

    i wish this map would show
the food my father devoured.
i could walk the whole of the island
for the good pelau   the bake   the roti.
these meals melt from mountainsides
and i don't know where they grow.
can i ever taste their salty steam
wafting from my own stovetop,
if i don't know where they grow?

    i wish this map would show
where the queer girls go. in places
of pretending those girls don't exist,

they hold each other
somewhere, perhaps in plain sight.
perhaps they are the intertwined vines
slipping through the seams of buildings.
as i reach for a stem,
firm fingers grasp my hand.

    i wish this map would show
       home.
show me why my throat sings
a distorted, distant echo of calypso,
why Trinidad's mosquitoes inflate me,
trying to resuscitate my dry, dulled skin,
why guidebooks detail trails for tourists,
but no passages to revival
for the island's daughters.

this is not a map
for finding myself, no,
but i know where i am not.
there are no lines drawn by hand.
there are no parachutes
to carry me gently home.

Trini Talk

Once, I knew
my father's voice
as his own tune.

Then came school.
With class in session,
I got the words right.

In the right place,
in the right order,
with the right sound.

Now, I heard why people
asked about an accent
in my father's tune.

He treated his words
like a child's balloons,
floating them into the air,

ending with vowels,
taking care to avoid landing
on anything sharp.

In school, they said
nothing about Trini talk,
nothing about language

neither right nor wrong,
so I came home

and tried to help,

to point out where
he was wrong and say,
Daddy, say it right.

No, I knew nothing
of Trini talk, or I'd have asked
to share that song.

Teach me come
to de words
with an open mouth.

Teach me say Calypso
just so, like we limin'
'til de sun goh down.

And teach me how dis tongue
can find mih home,
find me freedom.

No matter who say
we talkin' wrong,
cut eye doh kill.

No matter who say we wrong,
we come from someplace right,
and from dat place we come strong.

where the marble goes

we don't know
where the marble landed
we do know this yard where it last tumbled
so we know it will remain where it rests
no matter   i guess   that it's my favorite marble
orange like the fish i kept for two whole weeks
and purple like the last birthday dress mom made me
it's gone because my brother said so   and he's
always right   and he's watching   for the marble   i
think
frowning eyes following some kind of smoke trail
the yard looks all rusted up   even the grass
seems like it's growing old wheelbarrows
and torn tin cans   there's a neighborhood watch
sticker
on the fence in the driveway sits a sheriff's car
just like every weekend   i say *maybe*
he's not so bad   that's my best marble
i say   *maybe he'll help us get it back*
there's a click in the yard   i don't know
what from   but my brother says
we have to go   now   and my brother's
always right

Hushed

We held our breath through any tunnel,
heading home, to school,
on field trips to the zoo.

All of us did it, dozens of kids
stopping our squealing,
backs straight against battered black seats
as shade engulfed the bus.

All of us did it for luck, I suppose.
No word on what we were to do
with our collected luck,
or what it meant if one kid,
giddy and dizzy, sprinkled giggles
through the rows of us.

My dad once spoke of angels.
He talked about his elementary school,
where nuns taught in long rooms
open to streaming sound and sun.
In rare moments, the whole school
seized the same instant to catch a breath.
They used to say, in that moment,
an angel passed above.

How did new drivers account
for the hush on the bus?
Did they turn to see the still, silent children?
In the legends they learned, what creature glided
overhead?

7

mr. lowell's religion class, st. mary's high school

i knew the answer
to the true or false question,
and i knew *my* answer—
the two were not the same.
the question of eternal damnation,
cut down to two lines of black words
darkening the white sheet
on my desk. mr. lowell
would mark it correct if i placed
myself among the condemned—
it didn't say so, not exactly,
but if his church's communion
would unlock the gates of heaven,
then the key remained far from my reach.
mr. lowell stood under the flag pole
by the door, so lean, so pious,
i once tried to peek through
his clouded door at lunchtime
to see if he ate anything more
than leaf-thin communion wafers.
and so tall, taller still, it seemed,
when he spoke to us but not
at us, his eyes lifted to the ceiling
as if he stood directly below god,
asking for approval. god sat at the edge
of my desk, her gray dreadlocks
dipped in ink black as my pupils.
she moved a lock to circle
the wrong answer, *my* answer.
afraid mr. lowell would see her,

and bottle her up in the bulbs above,
i swatted her aside, and marked
the answer that damned me—

true.

or was it false?

Before We Know

it is before we know why bodies that touch
blaze with fire both warm as home
and searing as danger.
it is when we amble about on long doe legs,
thin and graceless as a newborn fawn's,
and our breasts aren't more than buds.

we don't yet know what sexy is
but we learn what it is not –
your hair, when kinky (now
is when you learn to use
your mother's straightening comb),
my obsidian lips, too dark, too full.

before the mirror we declare
what we are not – your mother's
funny dishes, the curry and the callaloo,
my father's funny way of saying *r*s.
i'm blowing kisses at the mirror,
wearing too-red lipstick. not yet knowing

what sexy is, but with each kiss,
drawing closer.

Shades of Nude

that time at the department store, when
i asked the sales girl to repeat herself,
not the part about the bra's price or size,
but the part about the color,
she licked her lips before she said,
it's nude. you know. like flesh.

the bra was white sand on my skin,
no flesh of mine, and if i could go back
i'd rise to the chance to tell her
what she's missing under that pale
ceiling with the bright white lights,
tell her about the shades of nude outside,

flesh colored like raw earth after rain,
skin hardened like the trunk of a redwood tree,
opening to insides soft as the forest floor.
nude wraps more firmly around bodies
without rest, and drapes more softly
upon those bare and beaten. remember these bodies.

we cannot all blend with your bras or cover up
with your cover-up. color me colorless, if you
think you can, but the stories on my skin
won't erase with your paint or fall to your fabric.
i'll take the brown one, was all i said,
while my aching body shook for more.

remember tonight

remember tonight,
something you haven't in a while:
that time in ninth grade ,
when you broke up with kenneth meyer,
and he yelled *dyke!* at you from the car
as his mother drove away.
you didn't understand then,
but you get it now. it's the way your
eyes follow a woman's walk, the
way your gaze answers some silent
call from hips like the ones resting
on your couch now.

remember tonight,
the elegance of the woman sitting
in your living room. she has a striking
allure, the woman on your couch,
so it's only natural that you are hiding
in the bathroom. turn on the faucet, knowing
you've already been hiding too long.
if the rest of this night follows the path
set by your dancing, tonight
will be your first night
making love, or something like it,
to a woman.

remember tonight,
with relief, that you shaved your legs
this morning, as you imagine the woman
stroking your bare thigh. then, that you gave up

12

before you finished, shaved your whole left leg,
but only your right ankle
before you decided to wear long pants.

tonight, remember this:
if she touches your thigh, let it be your
left one. as you tie your hair up with a band,
wonder if the woman can tell by looking at you
that every orgasm you've ever had
has been an over-gasped lie.
maybe you've had enough practice to fool her, too.
open the bathroom door to see her sitting
across from you, waiting, watching.
her eyes look black as her hair, beneath silver bangs.
eyes you can't keep secrets from.
sitting beside her now, you're not as sure
as you should be.

remember tonight,
your time at school, how they treated girls like you—
now, you can say *girls like us.*
your life is not like this woman's, choices made
simply.
you can't toss away your past as easily
as her thin white shirt, or put your cold hand
on a stranger's chin and turn her face to see you nude.
the woman's chest rests under more shadows
than light, but you can see she has just one breast.
if you didn't know any better, you would
think it was her heart, that flesh hung outside
of her body like a flag, proof that she's not all hollow
on the inside. on the opposite side of her chest

is a labyrinth of hardened skin.
no promises for peace of mind
when you reach the center.
she asks if you've ever been with a woman
with one breast before, and you pause, breathing
deeply, as though it's something you have to try to

remember, tonight,
before you tell her no.
of course, you've never been with a woman
with two breasts either, and you might think
it'd be easier to manage one breast
than two. you would be wrong.
put one hand over her full breast.
terrified of what your fingers might say
to the other side, let your tongue do the talking.
you never thought she'd taste like this.
like the smoldering ash marking where the fire has
burned.

remember tonight,
the stories that sliced your scars,
and know she's no different than the rest of us.
agreed to let her scars stay
as long as they gave her strength.

remember tonight,
what you sacrificed to get here.
then leave that to yesterday
and remember tonight.

the people say

black girls don't do yoga,
so we'll call this a stretch
of her impossible imagination,
another way her brain eludes the limits
of her brown body's available shapes.
where is the anger in her breath
when her exhale mends the fractured frame
preserving the form of her clay?
how can she sigh so light,
inhale and bend, while her sisters and brothers
divide from their own silhouettes,
rays shining behind them
but never illuminating their chests?

who does she think she is?

the people say
        she think she special.
but she never will be.

hear them say
        she tryna pretend she don't have problems,
and maybe she is.

though she knows the wood she stands on
once swung strange fruit with her shadow,
her limbs remember moving
to crease the curses stuck
to her history books' covers.
no, black girls don't do yoga,

15

and black girls don't breathe deep.

too shallow is the air she sinks into at birth.
too frantic, the footsteps she's grown to follow.
she can't exist in the pause of the present
with existence spinning
on the need for escape.
easier to picture her stillness as an accident,
to think she's sprawled to see
the outer circles of her reach,
her lungs infused with a resuscitating life force.
must we also see the only breath
come to save her on this flat, brown plateau,
flowing from the depth of lungs all her own

Deviance

I've stayed in the front yard all my life.
I want a peek at the back
Where it's rough and untended and hungry weed
grows.
A girl gets sick of a rose.

Gwendolyn Brooks, *a song in the front yard*

define desire

i'm saving your place beside me
while you're out casting your desire on a wire
with pick-up lines you toss out and reel back
and press up against your life-vested chest.
have you ever wondered
what else you could pick up
with your fisherman's hands?

stop and pick up my groceries, maybe.
after all, what is desire, if not hunger?
the emptiness of yearning,
picturing the weight of morsels on the tongue
with every breath of waiting.

i wish you would pick up the pace,
quicken the beat of your steps
when you're heading my way.
what is desire, if not a song of silence?
wishes whispered between words,
sighs caught between confessions,
and the impossible distance between
the start of your dive into me
and the welcome rupture of my shell.

i bet you can pick up just about anything
you set your mind to carry.
but what is desire, if not a trembling hand?
fingers fluttering like wet wings
skimming the stirred surface of a gray blue lake.

18

try to pick up your tone
at your sentences' end.
what is desire, if not a question?
        may i?
                may i?
                        may i?
        please?
each one born of the unholy union
of doubt and faith.

do you really believe your pick up lines?
do you believe
like i believe in you,
and do you hold your breath between
casting a line and feeling a tug,
like i do between reaching out and meeting your
touch?

once you've come back within reach
i'll ask you what you think—
what is desire, if not some kind of wire
leading back to the place i've saved for you?

Perks

Boobs will get you out of speeding tickets.
When the police officer sidles up to your car
with his pink fingers on his belt,
you'll see, in the glisten of his shades,
he's at just the right angle to peer down
and forgive your recklessness.

Boobs will get you free drinks at the bar.
Conversation's not necessary.
The music's too loud,
but a giggle that sends a jiggle
through your rack
will say enough, and more.

Boobs will use their power
even if you try to cover them up.
There aren't enough layers of fabric
to quiet the call pulsing from your chest.

Boobs can help you make friends, easy.
You don't even have to share names.
And you don't have to worry
about hoping for ears to perk up
for what you have to say.

natural colors

we decide your bedroom needs more
natural colors, after we've spent the morning
confronting your white male privilege
in just those terms. you are sure
i'm tracing our histories because i care enough
to broaden your world. i don't tell you
i'm just afraid what i did with you last night
was some anti-feminist blunder.

we spend the afternoon painting your walls
the colors of the rainforest, though somehow
they grow more brown than green. we can only
laugh at our efforts, when we have more paint
on ourselves than on the walls, when i trip on a can
and create a brown pond on the floor, when our
bodies
become bare as i roll my natural colors
around your floorboards.

now, i am more.
more than the paint on your walls,
than the blink dividing your thighs.
mine isn't the first brown body you've seen.
it's just the first time brown surrounds you,
and your body burns in solitude.

so when the paint has dried, and my pores
are ghost prints on the floor, i dare you
to look at the colors there, and find
me here once more.

Change of Night

Am I to be cursed forever with becoming
somebody else on the way to myself?
                    'Change of Season,' Audre Lorde

There is a woman who gazes from my mirror only
when night is coming.
Even without the darkening sky, I'd know, by the
flicker in the glass, night is coming.

With rushing fingers, I speak to my pores, to my
scalp, to the beds of my
nails and to all of my roots. I tell them night is
coming.

I sit at the bathroom sink, cream clay in one hand,
water at the fingertips
of the other. Never sure whether to cleanse my face
or cover it when night is coming.

Like a rat sensing the rush of water, I scurry to higher
ground. From my rooftop, I can always
find a parallel solitude. Tonight, a woman sips coffee
as if she doesn't know night is coming.

I think I'm getting older, for I've begun to worry
when I hear no worry.
Mom hasn't yet called to see that I'm safely home,
and night is coming.

22

Let's pretend we can lock our doors and close our windows to keep the terrors out.
Let's pretend our fears crawl to life only when night is coming.

Here is a change to relive each day – the rebirth of night.
Be reborn in darkness – night is coming.

what i meant to say

i made her a promise i couldn't keep.
knowing that didn't stop me from trying,
stumbling over every *forever*
before falling to rest with my head between her
breasts.
maybe all i meant to say was *i feel comfortable here,
right now.* but it came out sounding like a vow.

our first time was my first time
taking a woman's virginity,
though i didn't know it
until she hummed something like,
i've never done that before,
and i said, *huh?*
when i meant to say,
what the fuck?
when she said,
wow, i'm not a virgin anymore,
i said it again, *huh?*
when i meant to say,
what in the actual fuck?

i should've known,
when she was digging through me
like my pussy was a thrift store sale bin.
i should've known
when she stopped and gasped,
i can't find your clit,
though i didn't know she was trying,
or when she cooed

24

i see love in your eyes, or maybe
i've made love to your thighs?

and i wish i'd known,
before i tossed her around
like a swear word empty of its meaning,
hardly scandalous enough
to bring satisfaction as it clicks off the tongue.
if i'd known,
i might've recalled
that promise i made to myself
never to do a virgin
the way somebody once did me.

your cat speaks of sadness

attention, please. this is your cat speaking.
and i say it's time to snap out of it.
you've felt lifeless as a lump of litter,
sulking in bed like the world has lost
all of its string. you're forgetting
to connect with your pride of people,
and worse, you're forgetting about me.
if it meant only answering
your yowling cell phone,
you wouldn't need to be more
than this pile of blankets and sighs,
but now, this is your cat speaking,
and i say it's time to get out of bed.
i admit, you make a good cushion,
a plump pillow of trapped body heat,
but i've got other needs, you know,
and you won't even
raise a hand to scratch me,
won't lift your head to my meow,
won't even turn when i purr
to see why the hell i'm so happy.
well, i'm not. i'm not happy.
dammit, this is your cat speaking,
and to me it seems like someone's
clawed out all your stuffing.
i shove my face against your lips,
and find them dry as kibble.
and if i didn't know better,
i'd think you were crumbling,
but this is your cat speaking,

26

and i see you. i've seen you alone,
i've seen you nude, i've seen you
shielded by the armor of your solitude,
and i've seen you scooping my poop.
and maybe i'm just your cat speaking,
so i don't know much about your sadness,
but for me it's like this – i'm chasing a ball,
and it's skidding toward the fridge. i know
it's about to vanish into that dark abyss,
but do i try to stop it? no. i rush forward,
bat it along, and moments later,
i'm mewling for that lost ball.
now, i can always moan at the fridge,
can always paw underneath it,
and i'll know
that ball is down there somewhere,
just beyond my claw's reach.
so, stretch your arms like me,
and come on back to life –
please. this is your cat speaking,
and i say it's time to snap the hell out of it
and feed me.

Runaway

Or maybe my child has just run away.

I see her at five,
  filling a dulled orange bag
with her most-loved toys.
  In this version of things,
she cherishes model horses,
  like her mama did.

She carries one by its back legs
  as she starts up the street.
She looks over her shoulder, shivers
  to see our house fading to the fog.
She drops her horse
  and trots back to me.

Later, she'll tell me I nearly lost her. I'll say,
  You dropped Bo? He's your favorite horse.
We'll put on our coats and go out
  to bring Bo back together.
The horse's coat, color of a lucky penny,
  will shine from the street.

I see her again at fifteen,
  when I've grown to despise teenage boys
who stink of cigarette smoke,
  and she's grown
a fondness for them. She gets into a truck
  with one, ready to abandon town.

In this version of things,
   I sense her absence before I know she's gone.
On my way home, I call the school.
   My cell phone reception cuts out
as a woman tells me I shouldn't worry.
   My stomach gallops until I see her in the driveway.

She hugs me, crying,
   won't tell me what's wrong,
just says, *I dropped Bo.*
   Behind her, the boy with the truck shrugs.
In this version of things,
   my child has words only I can hear.

mari goes home

i'm eating an apple and watching the neighbors move
when you tell me they're not the only ones leaving.
man and wife share each load, lifting bookshelves and
bed frames together. it won't be like that for us. you'll
go
the way you came, with piles of paint-splattered
knick-knacks beneath a slick blue tarp in the bed of
your red truck.

will you leave wearing the same smile you brought to
me,
your chest held high as you move forward? you're
going
home to detroit. i've been there once, and i don't
know
why you'd trade me for hollowed warehouses encased
in a breathless atmosphere. i can't ask, so i gnaw
my apple 'til its center splits, broken bones in my
teeth.

how are we to know how this goes? i never watched
my mother wave a lover down a long road, didn't
grow up with any mention of how one woman sends
another off without the absence chopping her down.
without becoming a lone tree falling. no sound.
yet you stand steady, as if you've seen this all before.

i thought i'd be the one to go home or someplace
like it, thought my family stayed on a far-away
island because someday i'd need to leave this land

30

and all who treat my feet as fixed roots. here i stand
now, afraid you'll rip my roots from their beds. more
afraid
of what will grow when you leave than of withering if
i stay.

island home

well, wouldn't you be afraid?
if memories slipped from your skull
like the warm sand of your island home
falling through the cracks in your brain,
while you clutch all you have left by your ribs
in your sleep, waking each morning
to find someone tugging your treasures away.

this is for Granny A,
who's beginning to forget.
she's forgetting my father's name,
and the name of the island she calls home,
the place the rest of us call Trinidad,
only because we haven't lived as long as she has—
lived there so long she doesn't need to call the island
by name,
can reach out to it the same way you can call the
mosquitoes,
by dripping sweat like syrup, not salty but sweet,
from sugar cane thicker than your thigh.

it's no wonder she doesn't want to change her
clothes,
when the folks who offer new outfits
look more like strangers each day,
and the only thing more familiar
than the warm, thick blanket of heat
is her own smell, rising from her body
so that each time she inhales,
there's a chance she could take back

something once within her,
like echoes of her babies' cries,
which once leapt from the walls of this house
as she wondered if they'd come from her own throat.

some parts of the island will never leave her—
the open air's curl of her hair,
the stray dogs who follow on her heels.
in a way, one can never get lost
beneath skies made of honey and cantaloupe stains,
and in a way, even the unpaved roads
will always lead home.

you don't remember,
but you've been there before.
all of us have been there,
with strangers doing for us
what we can't for ourselves,
but Granny A is holding on
in a way we don't know how.

so, i say this for my grandmother,
who's thinning but not waning,
who might've spoken up herself,
but she's not like me.
it's not words she wants to remember.
so while I stand so far from her island,
trying to decide where on my body I will fit tattoos
of all the words I never want to forget,
she's kissing and tasting each memory
as it floats on the wind drifting away.
and someday, she won't remember what home is,

but she'll know how it feels,
and she'll know,
on her lips, on her skin, and in her bones,
this is the air she wants to breathe.

the people say

black girls don't kiss dogs,
so we'll call this another one
of her heart's experiments,
and we'll clack our tongues
at the lack of limits on her love—
how she shows affection
to any creature, regardless
of slobber or shedding,
of scales or feathers or fur.
what kind of hole does she try to fill,
writhing through dirt
to utter her adoration
to an animal who can't answer?

what in God's name is wrong with her?

the people say
        white folks have pets in their beds.
and so does she.

hear them say
        the Lord gave us dominion,
but watch her share

her air, her bed sheets, her space,
and the warmth flowing through her,
with any four-legged thing
to crawl to her and cuddle.
no, black girls don't kiss dogs,
and black girls don't snuggle with cats,

and black girls don't bond with beings of other
species.

could this be a sign of surrender?
giving up on the humans
who shrug off her sighs
like they would the braying
of an overworked mule.
welcoming a commitment
unfamiliar to her own kind—
devotion
with unconditional terms.
or is the devotion all hers,
all open, discovering only animals
with the unwavering courage to absorb it?

After

She says this is our chance to live happily,
rather than pausing to await the hereafter.
With our walls growing from the roots of a sorrel
tree,
like magic, we build a rooftop from our laughter.

And I think, perhaps, we'll never go back to where
homes are built from melted stone and dead wood.
Here, she moves with purpose and steps with care,
leaves rocks where they rest, trees where they've long
stood.

Until the day I rest alone among the rocks
as she traces my steps down the trail that fades.
She follows my crumbs like they're doors to unlock.
Our home is forest again and our rooftop flies away.

Perhaps these stories aren't for women with appetites
like hers.
Perhaps I was alone all along, hearing the laughter of
firs.

The Bookseller

The old man
never remembered my name. He erupted
from within book stack volcanoes
each time I entered the shop, exclaiming,
Marsha! Or *Marcy!* Or *Missy!*
and offering tea.
I never took his names for me
but I took the tea, warm cup cradled
in my palm as I browsed the shelves
for misplaced poetry. He never kept
the words I wanted in the right place.

I'm just an old bookseller, he'd say,
his excuse for everything
from forgetting my name
to falling behind in technology trends.
No e-books around here.
I'd correct my name and he'd slap
his forehead, close his eyes, then tell me
I could look upstairs, if I wanted, even though
those books weren't on the shelves yet.
Even though I'd have to tip-toe,
because folks lived up there,
on the other side of the black door.

Some time has passed since I visited.
Today, I walk by and hand-printed signs
pour words down the windows.
Store closing. A day later, and I'd have
passed a padlock, dark windows,

and a farewell sign thanking
the neighborhood for thirty good years.

Today, I'm here just in time
to step inside once more. Quietly.
The bell that once announced my arrival
is already packed away. Today,
he doesn't bother with my name.
He looks at me as if I'll have the answer
when he asks, *Those folks upstairs –*
will they remember us? The way
our whispers rustle pages?
The way we tip-toe by their door?

Today, I'm here just in time.
He sets his clay teapot
to rest in a brown box,
and tucks the flaps together
like folded wings.

bus seats

let's be real – if we start out as strangers
seated side by side on this bus,
we may end up as enemies.
who knows what might happen
if the two of us share one bubble
in this shaking soda can?

you might reveal yourself to me
one sunflower seed at a time,
your overflow of snacks and spit
leaping dangerously close
to my side of the white plastic hump
that divides us.

or maybe you'll be weary enough
to fall asleep, your head hovering
above my shoulder like a bird
circling her kill, threatening to drop
right down into my personal space
the moment you drop from consciousness.

or you'll pick up your phone,
lean away from the rest of the passengers

as if to shield them from the dreary details
of your life, but talk directly into my ear.
i'll have enough information to recommend
that you take a vacation and stop speaking
to your mother, but i'll keep my mouth shut.

you might even dare to speak to me.
take it upon yourself to disrupt the scratch
of my pen on this page, to ask me what
i'm writing. ask me where i'm from.
you might even ask me if you can touch
my hair, and you know there's no turning back
once you've gone there.

but today, we won't get the chance to ride
together through the strangeness of strangers.
today, i must look to you like some kind of thug.
me, carrying only my gentle breath beneath
loose jeans and a baggy black sweatshirt.

i saw your light eyes scan the landscape here,
the crowded corners, the families smashed
together to share one seat. i saw your eyes stop
on the cold plastic beside me, and stay there
for one whole minute before you planted your feet
in the dark, sticky soil of the bus's floor,
deciding to stand rather than sit beside me.

so go on, stand. enjoy the ride,
as you sway with every turn
and stumble with every shudder
and i breathe a little bigger

and stretch out over the seat
you'll never claim as yours.

now, perhaps, we won't share
sunflower seeds or spit or sleep
or unwelcome speech.
and maybe we'll have no
real reason to be enemies.

but your standing feet divide us
by something we haven't yet faced.
and maybe we'll never have
the chance to give it a name.

Careful

Sometimes, we discussed the way he treated her.

Their relationship
never came up during house meetings,
or in any conversations in her company.

But sometimes, when it was just
the rest of us, our voices dropped—
our hushed permission to speak.

Cole: *Her arm swings in that sling
again.* Jess: *Do her weeps seep into your room,
too? And her bruises into your daydreams?*

When we talked this way,
we whispered her name.
Nobody uttered his.

When you visited,
you didn't leave my arm in a sling.
You were more careful.

No need for yelling when a silent strangle
would do, and bones could be bent
'til the moment before breaking.

Still, sometimes I heard my name in whispers.
When you weren't around,
nobody uttered yours.

Uprooted

If the wind had never wrenched her tree loose
by its roots, she would not have found
the scent of the earth beneath it, spiced
like the folds of her skin. Nor would she know
the texture of newly risen dirt, coiled and shy
to the touch of her toes. And she wouldn't
have a gap in the ground, just large enough
for her body to nestle where the tree once grew.
Still, these days, as she nestles, all she can do
is think of the tree. Think of it growing. Think of its
roots

Healing

conscious as bees,
to the finest changes of sound,
and shadow, sweat and heat, she knows what she is to
do

-Dionne Brand, *ossuary IV*

Note: La Diablesse, a figure from Trinidadian folklore, is thought to be a former slave. She roams at night, and lures a man deep into the woods, until he plunges into a ravine or falls prey to wild hogs.

La Diablesse Dares

Wild hogs screech. Shrill.
Your scalp shivers.

Me, I am colliding chains.

You hear rattling bones,
call them clattering coins.

You smell enticing musk
of a darkening dusk

submitting to night. Cloth falls.

Wild hogs know you're not so hard,
your flesh not as hard as teeth.

Me, I wonder
if you'll follow,

then, how long you'll follow

white ruffles billowing my dress—
into the grip of darkness?

Until the coals of my eyes burn yours,
when you, peeking beneath my hat's brim,

spy upon what's left of me?

La Diablesse Ushers Dusk

Not resurrecting—
not exactly.
Not haunting. No.
And I don't simply slip out
from the saturation of thick air.

I come to you, lonely boy,
from gone-by days.
Hear the iron chains
slide across my waist,
and hear me rocking across the sea
to tend the fields as a slave.

Can't call me a ghost
if I still have my bones,
and I still have them stirring in my bag.
Stirring the dirt from my grave.

Unlike you, lonely boy,
I need no skeleton to carry my body.
For that, I have one hoof
stamping below my skirt.
Wouldn't you like to know
how a woman, so old, can return?

What'd your granny tell you?
Did she say I stop a solitary man
who's been doing wrong at dusk?
Then why you, lonely boy?
What you done wrong?

48

Watch your shadow.
Bet your granny's told you I'll take it.
Turn from the setting sun.
I'd say I already have.

chapped lips

my mind catches unwanted sounds.
it spins in spirals, repeating
the exact pitches of screeches and screams.
and i swear at least once a day,
a passing car or an open bar
tosses a pop song at me,
and i can't get that foolish four-note melody
out of my head, no matter how i try.

but i don't know how your mouth got up there,
stuck stiff inside my brain.
i hear not a sound coming from it,
but in the wood around doorways,
i see the ridges etched in your lips.
and in black grates over windows,
i see the alleys between your teeth.

and sometimes,
i hear the sound you made.
i've tried looking myself in the mirror
to say what you said.
turns out no other phrase
but *fucking nigger dyke*
carves your mouth
in so rigid a stance
around the hole it harbors.

no wonder
your mouth
is unshifting stone

50

settling in my mind.

the only sign of life—
pink skin blooming
from beneath concrete gray.
the surface of your lips was broken.
the new layers, raw.
i know how that feels.

Every Sunday

Does the black church keep black women single?
-2010 CNN headline

Sister Denise opens her Sunday closet.
She removes her Sunday clothes,
hat first, smoothing the blue brim
and coiling the ribbon before
it rests in its box. Blue skirt, blue blouse,
stiff from ironing, lift away,
as paper doll clothing. She unwraps
the panty hose scroll from her leg,
slowly, like her skin is sacred text.
Jewelry follows, pearls rolling
with the damp warmth of her neck.
She smells of thick floral perfume,
even without the clothes that caught
the scent from cardboard fans.
From her closet, a cotton gown.
Fabric falls loose as curtains,
so her body can breathe.
From bedroom to hall to den,
Sister Denise walks with her toes
wriggling in the carpet. She sits
in her rocking chair, closes her eyes,
the whirr of the air on her ear.
Soon, she'll start the cornbread,
and honey will sweeten the smell
of her skin and the quiet of her home.
The only voice Sister Denise wants—

the one on her breath as she sighs,
Thank you, Jesus.

Nightly

At midnight, they'll send her home early, once more.
And when she counts her ones, she'll find five
missing, once more.

She'll always choose the corner booth, if only because
of habit –
the waitress's habit of glancing over, once, twice, and
once more.

Juke box quarters sing to her, silver smooth-voiced
things,
saying, *Don't buy no more coffee, just play me that song, once
more.*

She'll drift down these streets, free as if she had no
home, feet bare
as if she had no shoes. She'll wander 'til the sun burns
its warning once more.

No one told her the nightmares would seize her at
daytime.
Waiting for her to close her eyes and lose herself,
once more.

Promises hurled like tabloid newspapers; the urgency
of uncertain truth.
Promises rotting like forgotten fruit; wondering who
to trust, once more.

She'll come back at sundown, to collect more dollar

bills. She'll find a note on her door –
Anita, I'll take care of you. Come back to me. And she'll
feed it to the gutter, once more.

this is not about birth control

a white man has my uterus.

perhaps i should be more clear.
    my uterus is inside the body
of a man, a man who works
    as a u.s. senator. so, i suppose
my uterus now spends
    most of her time behind
the beige buttons of a suit
    sitting in a big, white building.

i don't know how she got there.
    i know she's not resting
comfortably. part of her flesh
    weaves between the senator's ribs,
and another stretches around his kidneys
    as she tries to fit in with his organs.

he knows she's there, of course.
    at first, he tried to pretend
she wasn't. he told his wife
    it was indigestion that had him
lurching about all night,
    and when his young son caught him
wrapping his arms around his belly,
    he shivered and said he was cold.

soon, he learned to boast about her.
    he saw his secretary swallowing midol
and said, hey, i got one of them

56

uteruses, too, and you don't see
me complaining! as she already knew,
    each day he leaned against
the back of his office door,
    his body bubbling with pain.

on a fishing trip, his good ol' boys
    snickered about the gripes of women.
he joined in, saying,
    they don't even have it that bad,
you know. i've got a uterus now,
    and i'll tell ya, it's more of a comfort
than anything. more than anything
    i've ever known. the other men
watched the tears polish his eyes.
    they didn't ask him to fish again.

though he was boastful,
    he stayed away from the media.
rumors of the senator with the uterus
    seeped into the tabloids,
and he began to cover his torso
    with a black sheet when he
encountered the glaring lights
    of photojournalists. this is a private
matter, he'd say to them.

he tried to say the same to me
    when i asked for my uterus,
so i had to remind him
    that a matter of my uterus
is a matter of *mine*.

he was impossible to reach, at first.
i tried calling, and his secretary sighed
   when she relayed the words,
leave your uterus with me.
   you weren't taking care of her,
anyway. insulted,
   i wrote letters, tried to insult him
right back, but they all appeared
   in my mailbox with notes:
return to sender,
   and tell her to leave me alone.

emptier each day,
   i resorted to protesting outside
his office. other women were there,
   calling for the ends of wars
and for adequate healthcare
   and all. i held up only
one handwritten sign. it said,
   i just want my uterus back.

once, the senator agreed
   to return her,
when i threatened to take
   my story to oprah winfrey.
instead, i received a video
   from his wife. it shows
the senator on his mahogany floor.
   he's curled up, eyes closed,
like a newborn kitten. he's clutching
   his stomach, mewling, don't make me
send her away. his wife and two small children

58

stand in the background.
she covers their son's eyes, but lets
   their daughter watch. won't you
please let him keep her? she asked
   in a letter. he's gotten
so attached, and i don't know
   what he'll do without your uterus.

last i heard from the senator,
   he planned to give me what's mine.
i don't need your stinkin' uterus,
   he said on the phone,
sniffling.
   you'll get it in a few days.

twenty-eight days have gone by,
   and i still don't have my uterus.
the senator's phone is disconnected.
   news reports say he's resigned.
i don't sleep at night.
   i hold the hole at my center
and wait.

the people say

black girls don't have eating disorders
so we'll call this her *issue* with food,
the way she waits
for the closed fist of hunger
to clench under her ribs.
that empty mess—
her body's punishment,
whipping her from inside.
food becomes a trespasser on the tongue.
her belly's yearning will yield the reward
of looking a little more like skin
on skeletal remains.
such a look wouldn't be natural,

but isn't she *unnatural* in so many ways?

the people say
        she tryna be a white girl
but she never will be.

hear them say
        she tryna be cute
but she never will be.

no, black girls don't diet
and black girls don't have eating disorders,
and she's beginning to wonder, too,
if black girls don't hear *beautiful.*
if the best she'll hear is
cute, for a black girl

strike her passing backside.

she'll soon lose track
of this discipline's aim,
wandering through the wanting
without a compass to recall
what ignited the searching,
and what extinguishes
the searching's spark.
does she hope
for certain digits on the scale,
or for the emptiness,
just the company
of the emptiness itself?

juvenile inmate #1134

the first time she sees my tattoos,
she thinks she's discovered my secrets—
former gang affiliations,
scrawled in everlasting ink across my arms.
i tell her, *it's poetry,*
and her voice is my echo.
she adds, *i write poetry!*
as she hovers her face near my arms,
as if she might find her own words there.

like me, she's fond of purple,
and each week she asks me
for something in our favorite hue.
i'm not allowed to bring her anything,
but she searches me anyway,
to see if i've somehow delivered.
she finds violet in my veins,
lilac on the edges of my ink.
we talk about purple's finest looks,
trying to put words to the range of shades.

i let her break a rule each week,
by opening my arms before i leave.
the hug lasts only as long
as the guard takes
to turn away,
only long enough for my breath
to stir the dark roots
sprouting from her scalp.
if i'm lucky, there's time enough

for me to breathe in
her baby powder scent.

at night, i see the letters on my arms
change shape, like shadow puppets
in the moonlight.
a capital O becomes a sun
setting in the crook of my elbow.
a double-s creates the wheels
of a bicycle, like the one she misses,
careening off my wrist.

from my shoulder,
deep purple spreads like floodwater.

i never can tell
if it's the shade i love most
or the one she sees in me.

getting this out of my system

this kid smells like something died in her diaper,
and she expects me to pull her closer,
wiggling like a worm in my arms,
helpless without my constant touch.
why would anyone *want* this? i wonder,
though the thought doesn't come to me naturally,
not like the way my skin registers the cold
and i wrap her in my sweater without thinking.
my disdain for parenthood dangles
from my mind, and i strain to maintain it.
my uncle passes, points at the baby—
careful, those things are contagious.
i tell him, *don't worry, i'm just*
getting this baby thing out of my system.
he chuckles. my laugh is hollow as a cave,
only an echo inside.
just when i think this kid must've reached
the ultimate peak of stench, spit-up spills
from her mouth to me. regurgitated,
the goo she eats is even more disgusting.
her mother, my cousin, materializes
in that sudden, ghostly way mothers do,
says she's sorry, floats off to get a towel.
the tv returns from commercial to the news—
three juveniles killed after one drove drunk.
my palm turns the baby's face so she can't see,
even though she doesn't understand.
here's another reason not to have kids,
not her fear, but my own. i'd want a kid of mine
to stay too young to know, too young

to get into a car cursed to become a coffin.
my cousin comes back,
lifts her child from my arms,
turns for the towel,
though i don't feel i need it.
already my hands have moved,
not to clean myself off, exactly,
but to cradle my chest, just so.

Letter to a boy who won't write back

for Trayvon Benjamin Martin, Feb. 5, 1995- Feb. 26, 2012

I'm writing to you
like I wrote to Oscar Grant,
and why do these letters
keep growing longer?
I start out thinking
I'll send this page to Emmett Till's
sobbing wet coffin,
but before I've finished
more boys are beside him
resting too early
in their graves.

We didn't send you there to die.
Your mama didn't send you there to die
and I know you never asked to be a martyr.
We aren't asking for more martyrs.
We've sacrificed more black boys
than we can count,
though there's not a single one
we could ever forget.

When your mama called you Trayvon
she wasn't naming an FBI case
or a social justice movement
or giving me a title for this letter, no,
she was naming her son.
And you did everything
you were supposed to do.

You cried and squirmed within
your soft new skin,
and when she looked at your face
for the first time, she couldn't have known
your days together
would end so soon.

Another black boy heard
the last moments of your life.
He's thirteen years old
and they say he still hears you
pleading in his sleep,
and they say he's not doing too well
in school these days,
because math don't come easy
when you've just learned
how short life can be
in a body dark as his.

They say you were carrying Skittles
when you died, but were you carrying
your black boy script?
See, there are rules to follow,
there are lines to say
to get through a life like this one.
Just say, no, sir, to the police officer,
just say, yes, ma'am, to your teachers,
and say, I don't want your damn purse!
to every white lady you pass on the street.
Maybe then we'll all feel a little safer,
right?

We're still adding lines to the script.
Maybe the version passed down to you
didn't tell you to watch
for the neighborhood watch.

How come when they're watching,
I'm afraid for every boy who looks anything like you,
no matter how softly his eyes peer
from beneath his hoodie?

When the neighbors are on watch
is it fear or is it hate
that crawls from their eyes
and looks out from mine?
Whatever it is, I don't want it.
But on nights like the night
when we lost you,
I'm not sure if I can keep it away.

These assholes always get away—
that's what he said to the police dispatcher
before he killed you. He said,
these assholes always get away.
And isn't it funny, now,
isn't it exactly what I'm thinking
when I look at that photo of him?

Trayvon, when I look at your picture,
the one passed around
like a vigil candle,
the only light on our faces,
the one you took with your hood

framing your head,
I can't meet your round brown
eyes with mine.
I think I'm afraid to see
that you'll never look back.

No matter where we go from here,
you'll never look back.

marching with my sisters

do you know my sisters?
i walk with them to the rally,
taking two steps for each one
of their high-heeled strides.

i've painted red words on my banner—
no more violence.
i speed up to keep up,
banner still unfolding.

no more

we didn't mean to march,
but when we step to mission street,
unfurling our signs,
our tempo hits the sidewalk,
steady as a bass line,
and our voices tune to one melody.
el pueblo, unido, jamás será vencido—
the people, united, will never be defeated.

the doctors who delivered them didn't know they
were my sisters.
those doctors declared,
with a slap and a grin,
es un niño.
none of those babies were boys.

they would grow
to sashay through soccer practice,

70

to find light and a mirror
and their mothers' mascara in the dark,
to peel the curse of puberty
from their faces with razors,
to cross borders,
to remember their home lands
by calling themselves by lively names
honoring their *abuelas*.

they would learn
to hold their lacquered nails like stones,
centered in the spiral of their fists,
to spread brown powder
across the blue of an eye socket bruise,
to call on their sisters
to help build their shields.

now, you know they are my sisters.

we didn't mean to march,
but when we step to mission street,
unfurling our signs,
our tempo hits the sidewalk,
steady as a bass line,
and our voices tune to one melody.
el pueblo, unido, jamás será vencido—
the people, united, will never be defeated.

passing a man with a camera,
i wonder what his photos are for.
for laughing at the mash-up
of broad shoulders and slender dress straps?

71

for a gender lesson
to offer his daughters,
who sit on their bikes,
black afros bedazzled with pink beads?

you see that? the man says.
they're standing up for freedom.
for the freedom to be who you are.

my sisters and i march on.

we didn't mean to march,
but when we step to mission street,
unfurling our signs,
our tempo hits the sidewalk,
steady as a bass line,
and our voices tune to one melody.
el pueblo, unido, jamás será vencido—
the people, united, will never be defeated.

belly song

belly belly
belly song

my lover says he loves my belly,
and i've begun to believe him,
though i just can't imagine why.

belly belly
belly wrong
belly bounce   belly rolls
belly belly belly strong

no part of me is more
misshapen,
misguided,
overgrown.

belly belly
belly breathless

rogue, extra flesh bubbles,
an unwelcome billow of mold.
sweat spills down my belly,
clear puddles filling up my folds.

belly bruised
belly burned
belly soothe
deep belly turn

past lovers found it easy
to sway me with a shove.
even when my flesh was
out of reach, a word
could burn my belly
with the boil of dread.

belly swell
belly baby
belly well
belly empty

his palms press the landscape
around my navel. wouldn't know
this empty room beneath his hands
once held life, if i hadn't said so.
wouldn't know all i lost,
if he hadn't listened.

belly breathe
belly rise
belly breathe
belly fall

by now, my lover's found
all my flesh. and he's found
my clear sweat. and he's found
the boiling fear in me.
his hands don't recoil from the heat.

belly breathe
deep belly breath

74

black nerd love

the night lulls by before your thigh sweeps mine.
from books in our laps stir bespectacled eyes.
we have to put down the w.e.b. du bois—
your double-consciousness knowledge turns me on.

we've got to know *this is black nerd love*.
and this love anchors me to thoughts of
what bell hooks wrote about wholeness.
no single part of me does your kiss miss.

slide books aside, don't wonder why i love literature,
moan without comparing our sounds to white
vernacular.
the only questions you ask about my hair
whisper through your fingers as you tug with sweet
care.

when i'm loving you, i rock my own truth.
don't wonder if my punk funk tunes kill the mood.
to this moment in time, we both came from so far,
found there's no one right mold for who we are.

so we touch as naturally as our hair grows in locks,
release ourselves from tight belts and striped socks.
i welcome you like a black character in my dearest
comic,
let you thumb through me for uses of the erotic.

our shadows stream shapes of *black nerd love*.
with bodies entwined, we both rise above

the self-hate growing on that racial mountain,
for respect we learned from aretha franklin.

and passion we learned from klingons.
some folks wonder what planet we've landed on,
but we know this earth was made for our loving,
seeds from africa grew to bloom our special
something.

this is about more than dark skin and glasses,
and it's deeper than the handprint shapes on our
asses.
it's not just having sex or having something in
common,
or explaining our identities without any problems.

how many of us are here inside this room?
i mean, there's the self inside me, and the one others
see, too.
but with you, i don't struggle to know where i stand.
this is black nerd love, and all four of your eyes can see
who i am.

women who love

i learned to love a woman here,
by hearing the beat of my heart
find the echo of water
drumming in the ground beneath us.
there is balance here—
every ebb has its flow,
every sunrise, a sunset,
so if i love a woman 'til
our world tilts on its side,
we won't be tilting long until
the earth brings us back to center.

i learned to love a woman
by moving toward her.
inside my muscles are memories
of the woman who carried me
and she who carried her
and the one who carried her.
from their blood floods
the rhythm of my walk.

i learned to love a woman
by looking in the mirror.
there i saw her,
her body and mind
reflecting my own,
her gaze never veering
from my eyes.

i learned to love a woman

by changing my fist
from the shape of a grenade
to the shape
the size
the pulse
of a beating heart.
   a beat
for every time
my anger meets silence.
   a beat
for every wall
i wish to knock down.
i wanted to fight fear
without losing
what i've learned from it,
so i learned to love a woman.

if we hurt each other here,
they will only be pains
of the growing kind.
we hold one another
like the soil hugging
our ever unfolding roots.

two women who love,
that's called a revolution,
our bodies turning
'til we face something new,
'til our shapes are all new,
and everything we touch
is ablaze with the hot clay
of unset stone.

78

there is a balance here—

so each time i lose,
i learn to love.
and each time i love,
i learn to see
the light of fire
in every footprint behind me.

Finesse'

Maisha Z. Johnson is writer and editor living in Oakland, CA. She has an MFA in Poetry from Pacific University and she studied creative writing at San Francisco State University. Maisha works at the intersections of creative arts, healing, and social change. She's also the author of *Through Your Own Words: 51 Writing Prompts for Healing and Self-Care,* as well as three poetry chapbooks: *Split Ears, Uprooted,* and *Queer As In.* Her work has been published in numerous journals, nominated twice for a Pushcart Prize, and won awards and competitions including Literary Death Match, The Lit Slam, and the Leo Litwak Award.

83

In *No Parachutes to Carry me Home*. Maisha Z. Johnson opens up a space of truth, vulnerability and grace that is welcoming even as, we, as visitors, encounter the fears, the anxieties and the deep questions about this woman's world in ways that resonate with our own questions. Few poets write about the scents and earthy aromas of our human bodies as precisely and evocatively as Maisha Z. Johnson. For her, scent is memory and memory is scent. There is, in her poetry, such authority of language, syntax and thought—yes, a great deal of tough, challenging thought. "There is a woman" she says, "who gazes from my mirror only when/ night is coming", and somehow, she allows us to stand beside her, to see, too, the reflection and the coming night and we don't feel like intruders, interlopers or voyeurs. There is a gift in this—a remarkable generosity of art. This is important accomplished poetry that lingers like memorable scents of our lives.

Kwame Dawes, author of *Duppy Conqueror: New and Selected Poems*

In Maisha Johnson's powerful debut collection, *No Parachutes To Carry Me Home*, we find poems that incite new insight, that inspire and conspire to awaken us from any present stupor. Johnson is a poet with the courage to dig deep, below the surface, below artifice, below the oft told, tired old fictions that lull and deaden to find deeper truths. As Johnson writes in her poem dedicated to Trayvon Martin, "No matter where we go from here/you'll never look back." She won't, nor, after reading this dynamic poetry, will we. In "Island Home" a tribute to her Trinidadian grandmother she writes "...someday she won't remember what home is but she'll know how it feels …this is the air she wants to breathe." This collection provides us with the air *we* need to breathe. Lucky for us that this exciting new poet provides us with fresh poetic oxygen. Breathe deep.

-Toni Mirosevich, author of *The Takeaway Bin* and
Queer Street

Maisha Johnson begins this book with lines from June Jordan: *we came and we come in a glory of darkness/ around the true reasons for sharing/ our dark and our beautiful name.* And this is an apt description of what these poems do. Maisha Johnson is a clear and articulate young poet who takes on an astonishing range of subjects, always grounding the large ideas in personal and vivid images. These are brave poems, full of anger, honesty, humor, and love.

-Ellen Bass, author of *Like a Beggar, The Human Line,*
and *Mules of Love*

OTHER PUNK HOSTAGE PRESS BOOKS

FRACTURED (2012) by Danny Baker

BETTER THAN A GUN IN A KNIFE FIGHT (2012) by A. Razor

THE DAUGHTERS OF BASTARDS (2012) by Iris Berry

DRAWN BLOOD: COLLECTED WORKS FROM D.B.P.LTD., 1985-1995 (2012) by A. Razor

IMPRESS (2012) by C.V.Auchterlonie

TOMORROW, YVONNE - POETRY & PROSE FOR SUICIDAL EGOISTS (2012) by Yvonne De la Vega

BEATEN UP BEATEN DOWN (2012) by A. Razor

MIRACLES OF THE BLOG: A SERIES (2012) by Carolyn Srygley-Moore

8TH & AGONY (2012) by Rich Ferguson

SMALL CATASTROPHES IN A BIG WORLD (2012) by A. Razor

UNTAMED (2013) by Jack Grisham

MOTH WING TEA (2013) by Dennis Cruz

HALF-CENTURY STATUS (2013) by A. Razor

SHOWGIRL CONFIDENTIAL (2013) by Pleasant Gehman

BLOOD MUSIC (2013) by Frank Reardon

FORTHCOMING BOOKS ON PUNK HOSTAGE PRESS

L.A. RIVER LULLABY (2015) by Iris Berry

LONGWINDED TALES OF A LOW PLAINS DRIFTER (2015) by A. Razor

EVERYTHING IS RADIANT BETWEEN THE HATES (2015) by Rich Ferguson

RAISED BY CRIMINALS (2015) by Michael Marcus

GOOD GIRLS GO TO HEAVEN, BAD GIRLS GO EVERYWHERE (2015) by Pleasant Gehman

DANGEROUS INTERSECTIONS (2015) by Annette Cruz

RAW (2015) by Cassandra Dallett

DRIVING ALL OF THE HORSES AT ONCE (2015) by Richard Modiano

NO APOLOGIES (2015) by Jessica Wilson Cardenas

THE BEAST IS WE (2015) by Dennis Cruz

DISGRACELAND (2015) by Iris Berry & Pleasant Gehman

AND THEN THE ACID KICKED IN (2015) by Carlye Archibeque

BORROWING SUGAR (2015) by Susan Hayden

BASTARD SONS OF ALPHABET CITY (2015) by Jon Hess

CONFESSIONS OF A FIRECRACKER (2016) by Angela Aguirre

21701331R00065

Made in the USA
Middletown, DE
11 July 2015